JUST EAT IT ALREADY!

An ABC Book for Future Foodies

WRITTEN & ILLUSTRATED BY TAMI BOYCE

ISBN: 978-1-7361586-1-6

Tami Boyce Design
Charleston, South Carolina

Edited by Susan Burlingame

DEDICATION

To Joey and Luke

Joey, you're the picky palate
who inspired this book!

Luke — my consulting chef and partner —
without you, I'd still be living on a
diet based of Pop Tarts and instant ramen.

is for

AVOCADO

[ah-vuh-kah-doh]

With lime juice and salt,
we're a silky delight!
When turned into guac,
you will love every bite!

is for

BASIL

[bay-zuhl]

King of the herbs,
I smell strong and sweet!
In Italian or Thai food,
my taste can't be beat!

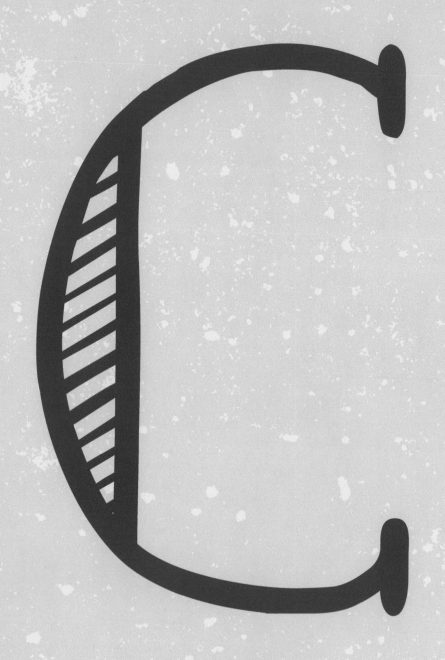

is for
CAULIFLOWER
[kah-lee-flah-wer]

Don't confuse me with Broccoli,
my brother-in-law.
Enjoy me roasted,
pickled, or raw!

is for

DAIKON

[di-kahn]

I'm a Japanese radish
with sweet, fresh flavor.
Toss me in stir-fries
you're looking to savor!

is for

EDAMAME

[eh-duh-mah-may]

I'm a young soybean
who's so fun to peel,
served in Asian restaurants
as a start to the meal!

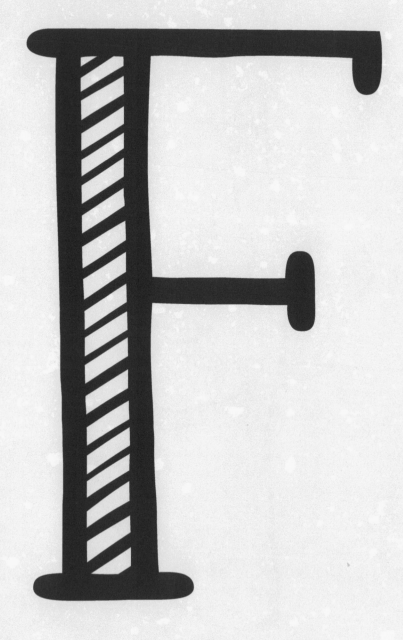

is for
FALAFEL
[fuh-lah-fuhl]

We're a Middle Eastern snack—
fried and *delish*!
Served crunchy and hot,
we make one tasty dish!

is for

GNOCCHI

[nyo-kee]

We're delightful dumplings
of fluffy potato,
We love a good sauce,
made from cream or tomato!

is for

HUMMUS

[huh-muhs]

A delicious dip made from
mashed-up chickpeas,
I like to be eaten
with pita or veggies!

is for

INCABERRY

[een-kuh-beh-ree]

I'm a superberry
with a taste that is yummy!
Eat me for health
and a satisfied tummy!

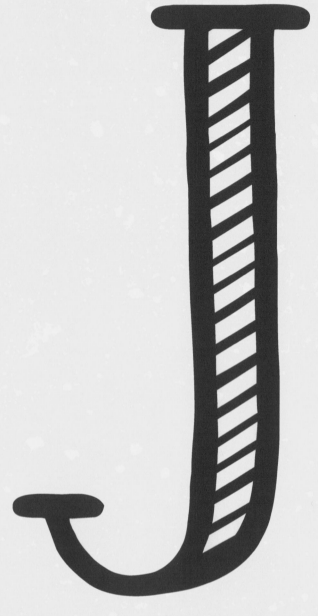

is for

JALAPEÑO
[hah-luh-peyn-yoh]

I'm a Mexican pepper,
and I'm hot; I won't lie.
You'll find it quite zippy,
if you give me a try!

is for
KALE
[kayl]

They call me a superfood;
for that, they're not wrong!
I pack lots of nutrients
to help keep you strong!

is for

LEEK

[leek]

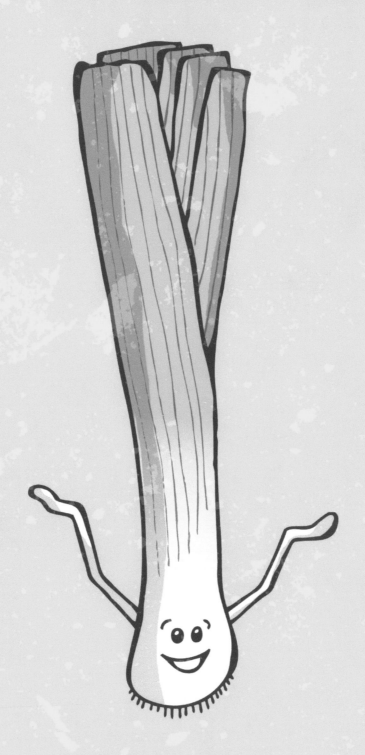

I'm kin to the onion,
but my flavor's more tame.
Cooks often use me
to up their chef game!

is for

MANGO

[mang-goh]

I'm a tropical fruit
with a colorful peel.
Try a big bite,
and you'll get the appeal!

is for

NAAN

[nahn]

All the way from India,
I'm a toasty flatbread.
If I'm on your plate,
you will love being fed!

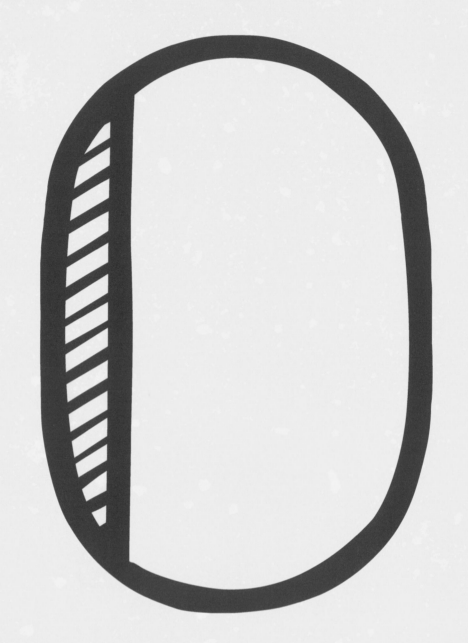

is for

OLIVE

[ah-liv]

I'm a bite-sized fella;
watch out for my pit!
On pizza or salads,
I'll be a huge hit!

is for

POMEGRANATE

[pah-muh-gra-nit]

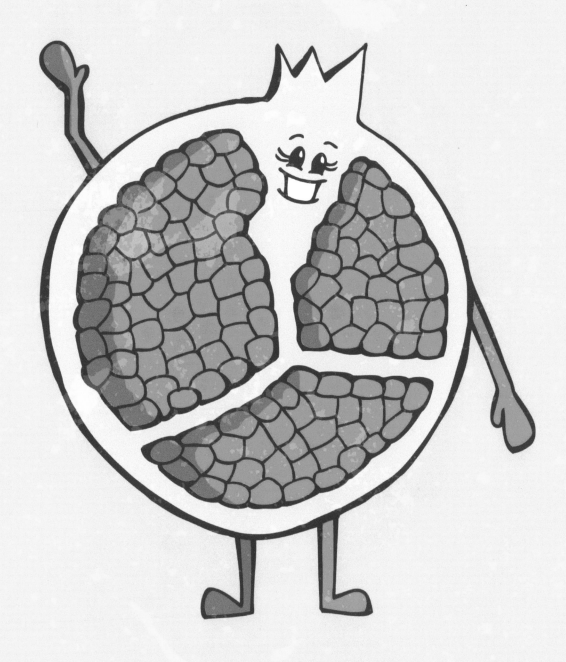

I'm a quirky red fruit;
it's my seeds that you eat.
They make a great juice
or a post-dinner treat!

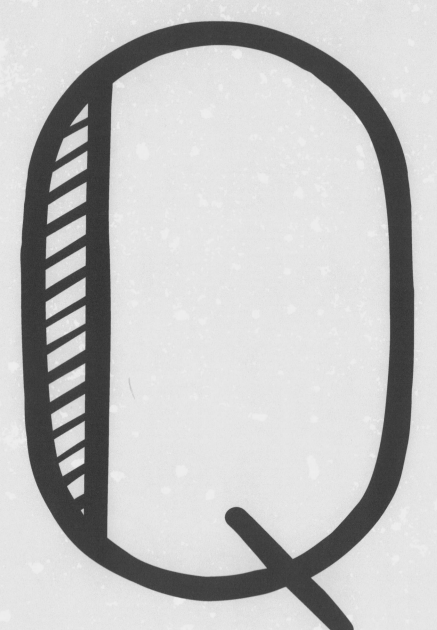

is for

QUINOA

[keen-wah]

I'm a seed full of protein,
and a fill-in for rice.
With sauces or veggies,
I can taste really nice!

is for
RHUBARB
[roo-bahrb]

My stalk can be tasty,
though my leaves you can't eat.
Bake me in pie
for a nice, tangy treat!

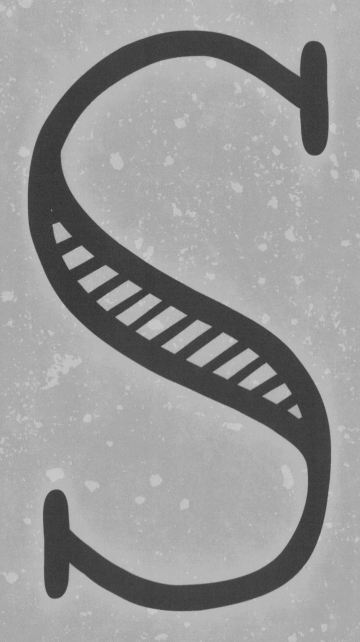

is for
SUCCOTASH
[suh-kuh-tash]

Mix shell beans with corn,
and I'm what you get!
Add in sweet peppers,
and now you're all set!

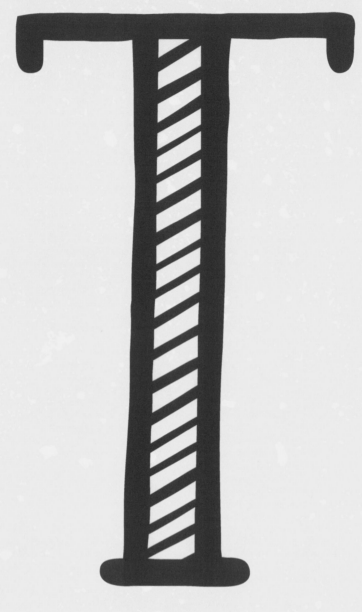

is for

TRUFFLE

[truh-fuhl]

I grow underground
like a buried treasure!
Chefs add me to pasta
for elegant pleasure!

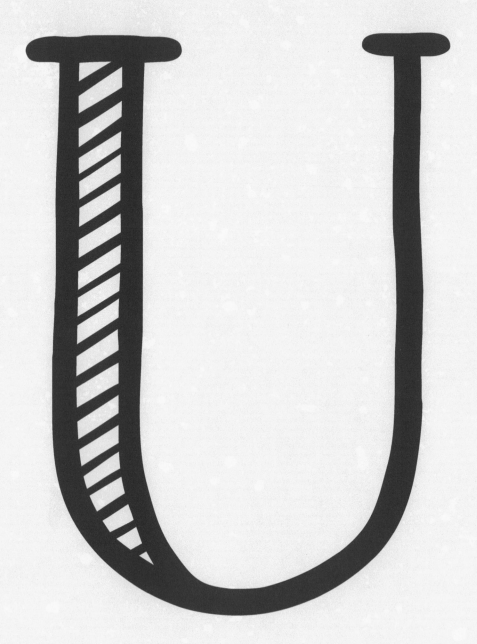

is for

UDON

[oo-dahn]

We're thick, yummy noodles,
enjoyed hot or cold.
Practice with chopsticks,
if you're feeling so bold!

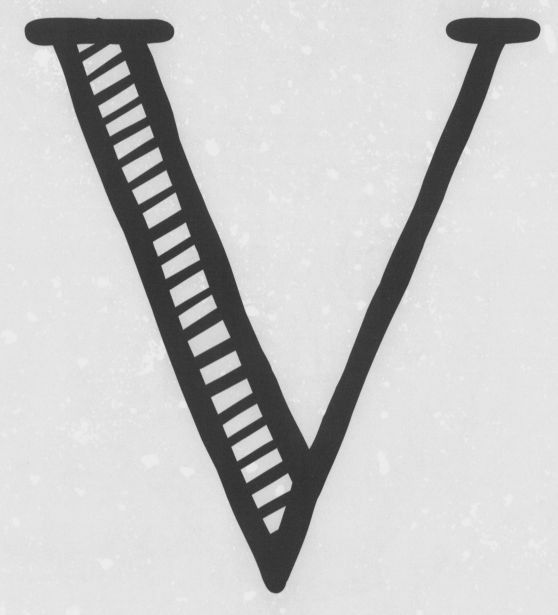

is for

VINAIGRETTE

[vih-nuh-gret]

Blend oil and vinegar—
that's how I'm made!
Enjoy me on salads
or as marinade!

is for

WONTON

[wahn-tahn]

I'm a Chinese dumpling
served boiled or fried!
I'm the part of the meal
you'll be glad you tried!

is for
XIGUA
[zig-wah]

You may likely know me
by my other name.
Xigua and *watermelon*
are one in the same!

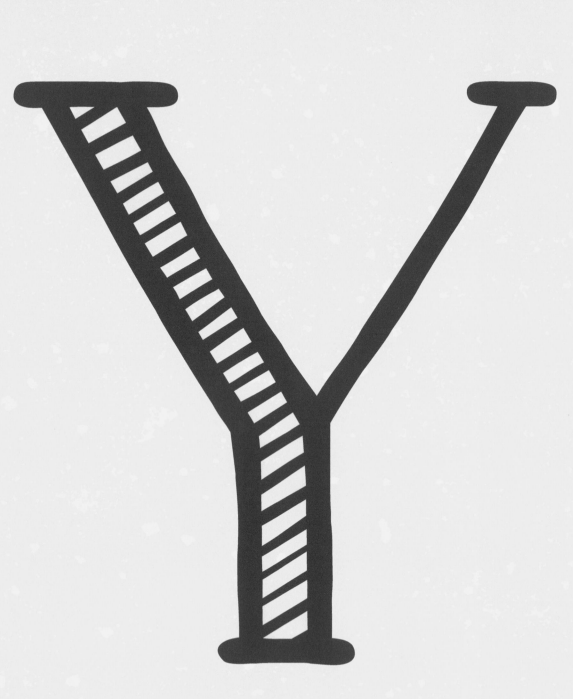

is for
YUZU
[yoo-zoo]

I'm a Japanese fruit,
with a citrusy taste.
When I accent a dish,
it won't go to waste!

is for
ZUCCHINI
[zoo-kee-nee]

A green summer squash,
I shine when I'm grilled!
Or try me in soup—
either way, you'll be thrilled!

MEET the AUTHOR and ILLUSTRATOR

TAMI BOYCE is an illustrator with a fun and whimsical style. Her work can be found at various establishments around Charleston, SC, including Theatre 99, Early Bird Diner, Frothy Beard Brewing, and the Station.

"Holding a pencil in my hand has been my passion for as long as I can remember. I count myself as an extremely lucky individual because I have been able to make a career out of it. We all live in a very serious world, and I like to use my quirky style to remind us of the love, joy, and humor that is often overlooked around us."

To see more of Tami's work, visit tamiboyce.com.

Photo by Leslie McKellar (leslieryannmckellar.com)

CPSIA information can be obtained
at www.ICGtesting.com
Printed in the USA
BVHW020933021220
594681BV00016B/160